CREDIT SCORE SECRETS

The Proven Guide To Increase Your Credit Score Once And For All. Manage Your Money, Your Personal Finance, And Your Debt To Achieve Financial Freedom Effortlessly.

DAVE ROBERT WARREN GRAHAM

This book is dedicated to those who, like me a few years ago, want to increase their credit score to improve their financial future.

Thanks to my wife and my children who made everything I have learned, possible. I achieved everything in my life with them and now… I can share it with you.

Good luck with your studies and your wealth! Enjoy!

Dave R. W. Graham

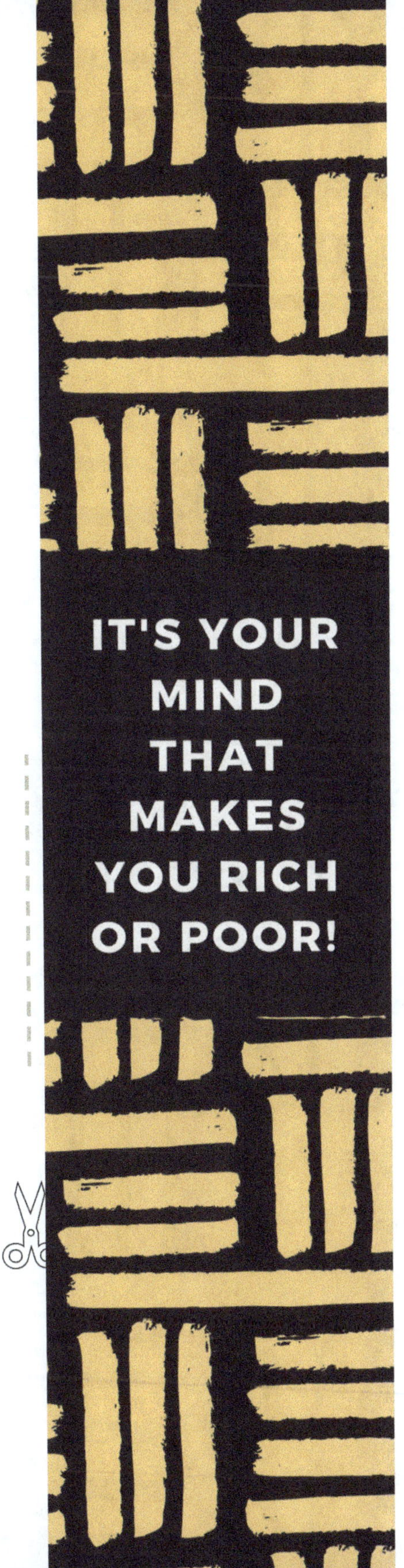

Control your
money or the
lack of it
will control
you!

A Gift For You

- Keep your audiobooks forever, even if you cancel your membership

… and much more

Just scan the QR code with your smartphone to get started right now FOR FREE!

Table of Contents

Let's get started

Introduction

In its simplest terms, a credit score is a number that represents your financial standing and is used by lenders (credit card companies, mortgage companies, auto loan companies, etc.). This number is determined by your current debt, your payment history, and your ability to pay off any debt in which you are trying to gain. Many other factors define a credit score, but this is the simplest way to explain it. An easy way to see how your credit score is shaped is by looking at the four main things they look at:

1. Who do you owe money to?

2. How much do you owe?

3. How much you have already paid?

4. How efficient are you in paying what you owe? (This is by far, the most important one)

One thing to note: There are multiple credit scoring models out there. What I have noticed is that most credit card companies tend to use a specific scoring model that affects certain loans, such as credit cards.

Failure is an experience that no one would like to go through. However, with a good plan and guidance, you will be able to overcome it.

If there are accounts or cards whose balance you have successfully paid out, do not close them. It is always good to view a clean criminal record. This phase has a triple advantage. First, it seems they have paid their debts. Secondly, it shows your expertise in paying more types of credit, and thirdly, it shows a more extended credit history.

This may not be explicitly mentioned anywhere, but it is just common sense. Increasing assets increases reliability. If you have sufficient resources, you will be able to mortgage them for credit. So, creditors will give you credit for getting a good guarantee in exchange for their risk. Avoid construction liabilities like credit card bills as they will affect your negative rating.

Always keep in touch with them and express your inability to pay, if that is the case, and see if it is possible to agree in any way. After all, they want their money and not the rating to fall.

10 Fundamental Reasons to Have Good Credit

1. Get funds to start or grow your business.
2. You will have access to money for emergencies.
3. You can qualify to buy a home and build equity.
4. Borrow unsecured money for college.
5. Access to reward programs that offer free travel.
6. Zero or low-interest auto loans.
7. No deposits on utilities and some leases.
8. Qualify for job opportunities that require decent credit and save thousands on insurance policies each year.

9. Purchase protection from merchants.

10. Travel protection and zero liability rental car insurance.

How to Improve Your Personal Finance: Managing Your Bad and Good Debt to Raise Your Incomes?

It's possible to improve your credit score. Your score is calculated using many different factors that carry different weights. The following is just some general advice on improving your score before we get into the specifics.The best thing that you can do to get your credit score up is to make payments on time. As soon as you start missing payments, your score will plummet. Delinquency can turn into a negative item that is much harder to remove. If you do miss payments, communicating and maintaining a good relationship with your creditor is critical. Having a broad mix of credit types on your report also helps to improve your score. Having five credit cards, for example, does not look as good as having two cards, an auto loan, a mortgage, and a student loan.

How Anyone Can Quickly Raise Their Credit Score

There are steps you can take to start increasing your credit rating.

Get a Copy of Your Credit Reports

Before you can work out how to boost your credit rating, you need to understand what score you are starting from. The first area you must go to boost your credit score is the credit report because of your credit rating based on the data in your credit file. A credit report is a listing of your repayment history, credit administration, and debt. It might also contain information regarding your accounts, which have gone into some other repossessions or bankruptcies and collections. Order copies of your credit reports from each of the three credit agencies to identify.

Dispute Credit Report Errors

Under the Fair Credit Reporting Act, you have the right. This right permits you to dispute credit report mistakes by writing to the credit agency, which has to investigate the dispute. Entrance snafus by lenders, identity theft, birthdays, or speeches, or readily interchangeable Social Security numbers, can hurt your credit rating. For Instance, if you possess a record of late payments reported since payments represent 35 % of your credit rating, payment on the record of somebody might have an immediate and dramatic effect on your score. The more quickly you get and dispute errors resolved, the sooner you can begin to raise your credit rating.

Prevent New Credit Card Purchases

New credit card purchases will increase your credit use rate—a %age of your credit card accounts to their credit limitations, which make 30 % of your credit rating up. You can calculate it. The higher your accounts are, the greater your credit use will be, and the higher your credit score might be influenced. It is better to maintain your credit use rate. In other words, you need to keep a balance of no more than $3,000 with a limit of 10,000 on a Credit card. Rather than placing them to decrease the influence to fulfill that goal, pay money for purchases. Prevent the purchase.

Pay off Past-Due Balances

Your payment history makes up 35 % of your credit rating, making it the most crucial determinant of your credit score. The further behind you are in your payments, the more it hurts your credit rating. As soon as you have curbed credit card spending, use the savings to have caught up in your credit card payments until they are billed (the grantor shuts off the accounts for future usage) or delivered to a collection service.

Do your best to cover outstanding accounts in total; the bank will then upgrade the account status to "paid in full" which will reveal more favorably on your credit compared to unpaid accounts. Moreover, by continued to take a balance as you pay off an account over the years, you will be subjected to finance fees that are continuing.

Be Patient and Persistent

Patience is used to calculate your credit rating, so it is something you have to have while you are fixing your credit score. So, don't expect it to increase in that period, your credit was not ruined immediately. Continue monitoring your credit, maintaining your spending in check, and paying for your debts on time every month, and over time, you will find a boost in your credit rating.

Pay off Debt

The amount of debt, which you are carrying as a %age of your credit, represents 30 % of your credit rating, which means you are going to need to begin paying down that debt. If you have a positive cash flow, then meaning you get more than you do owe, think about two procedures for paying.

Why Do You Have to Manage Your Credit Score?

Credit scores are essential tools that help you get approved for different loans such as a car loan, mortgage, or credit card. They show lenders if you can pay your loan payments on time. Additionally, it helps them decide the rates and terms for your loan, considering the associated risks.

With a good credit score, you could potentially save thousands and rent that apartment, or buy that house or car that you wanted, for less. Your credit scores aren't stored with your credit history (though the history of those loans and repayments stay on your report). These scores come up within a specific range every time a lender request for it.

Credit scores are therefore essential but aren't the only determinant for the rates and terms of your loan. Your credit history, on-time repayments, the total debt you accumulated over time, utility bill payments, and more are considered before you get a loan.

Chapter 1.

How to Get Started

Introducing Credit Score

Your credit score has an impact on credit applications in the future, so you want to get it as high as possible. A credit rating of good is the minimum you want to aim for if you want to be approved for credit and get advantageous interest rates quickly. FICO and Vantage Score both indicate that about two-thirds of Americans have a rating of good or better. This statistic shows promise for people who are attempting to build credit. It is not that difficult to do if you are careful with how you use your available credit.

An important aspect for some people is a minimum credit score. Technically, the minimum credit score a person can have is 300. You may often hear groups talking about a minimum credit score if you want to apply for an account or loan. The truth is that there's no such thing. You do not need to have a minimum credit score to apply for credit.

Mortgage providers (the companies providing credit for home loans) indicate that even people with low credit scores can apply for home loans.

The most significant difference is that you may not get favorable terms and reasonable interest rates if your credit score is poor. Many lending institutions require a minimum down payment of 10% and additional security if your credit score is below 580. In contrast, a credit score higher than 580 only requires a 3.5% down payment. This example clearly shows why a good credit score is better for people.

How Many Types of Credit Scores Are There?

Businesses have credit scores just like individuals, but the ratings work in a slightly different manner. You may be operating a business and need to take out a loan or purchase a vehicle on finance for company purposes. It is essential to understand the differences between good credit scores for businesses and that of individuals.

The most significant difference lies in the actual credit scores: business credit scores fall within a range of zero to 100. Similar rules still apply and the closer your business is to a score of 100, the better it will be for your credit applications.

The Experian score is broken down into more segments: high-risk businesses score 1 to 10; medium to high-risk score 11 – 25; the medium risk is obtained by businesses with a score of 26 to 50. The segments then become slightly more substantial. Businesses scoring between 51 and 75 pose a low to medium risk for lenders, and the lowest risk is when a business has a score of 76 to 100.

Equifax works slightly differently. They have one rating system for payment history and another for the likelihood that your business will fail. Instead of describing the scores in terms of risk, Equifax gives a ranking based on how you pay or how late your payment is to your creditors. Paying your creditors as agreed gives a score of 90–100; if you pay in the 30 days following the due date, then your score is 80–89. A score of 60–79 is attributed for payment 31 to 60 days after the due date. Paying creditors 61 to 90 days late will result in a 40–59 credit score; while a score of 20–39 is given for payment between days 91 and 120.

The non-FICO scores are called FAKO scores by some consumers. Experian has a credit score for educational use only (Plus Score) between 330 and 830, and Experian Scorex PLUS score is between 300 and 900. Equifax has the Equifax Credit Score between 280 and 850.

Some lenders use an Application Score between 100 and 990, and Credit Optics Score by ID Analytics Inc. between 1 and 999.

Several websites (Trans Union, Equifax, Credit Karma, Credit Sesame, etc.) offer different credit scores to consumers, but they are not used by lenders. Innovis, ChexSystems, and PRBC are other companies that produce credit scores used by some lenders.

Here's really all you need to know. You have a Vantage Score from each of the bureaus. They use the exact same formula because they all joined forces to create the formula. You would have the exact same Vantage Score from each bureau if you had the same information in each bureau. Although it's highly unlikely you have the same information in all the bureaus. The Vantage Score is used by only 10% of lenders. You also have a FICO score from each bureau. Used by 90% of credit lenders. This score would also be the same for each bureau if you had the same information in each bureau. This again is highly unlikely. You also have Industry Specific FICO Scores from each of the bureaus. Credit Cards, Auto Industry, Installment Loan, Personal Finance, and finally Mortgage.

Three Major Credit Bureaus, Three Credit Scores, Two Models Rating Agencies

Three main Credit Bureaus crunch the numbers and create a credit score that defines your score: Trans Union, Equifax, and Experian (there are in fact other companies, smaller ones, but these are the three we will focus on). Each Credit Bureau looks at different aspects of your financial profile. What this means is that, for example, Experian will take a heavy consideration of late credit card payments, but Equifax may not focus so much on that.

FICO vs. Vantage Scores

FICO Ratings

The ratings given by FICO are shown below along with the corresponding scores.

Fico Score	Rating	What the Score Means
300 – 579	Very poor	• Well below average • For a lender, you are a risky borrower
580 – 669	Fair	• Below average • Many lenders will approve loans
670 – 739	Good	• Near or slightly above average • Most lenders consider this a good score
740 – 799	Very Good	• Above average • You're a dependable borrower
800 – 850	Exceptional	• Well above average • You're an exceptional borrower

People with a credit score between 300 and 579 are said to have a very poor score; this does not mean that the person is financially poor. It is unlikely that these people will be approved for credit. If an application does succeed, then the applicant may need to pay a deposit or additional fee as security.

It is possible to improve this score through proper credit control and gain a better record. People with a good (670 – 739) credit score can easily obtain credit. Additionally, there is a very small chance for these individuals to start making poor credit decisions suddenly.

Most people want to be placed in the category of very good (740 – 799) or have a score of more than 800 to achieve the rating of exceptional. These individuals will be offered the best credit card deals from top lending companies. Another advantage of a high credit score is that you will be given low-interest rates when borrowing money.

Vantage Score Ratings

The Vantage Score ratings are slightly different as seen in the following table.

Vantage Score	Rating	What the Score Means
300 – 499	Very poor	• It will be difficult to get credit
500 – 600	Poor	• Some institutions will approve small amounts of credit with high-interest rates
601 – 660	Fair	• Some institutions will approve credit more easily but with high-interest rates

661 – 780	Good	• You will get credit more easily with competitive interest rates
781 – 850	Excellent	• You will get credit with favorable interest rates from some of the top lending companies

Vantage Score has an evener distribution of scores across the range. Those with very poor scores (300–499) have almost no chance of being approved for credit. These people will find it difficult to get credit and struggle to improve the score.

People with a poor (500–600) score might get a small amount of credit from some institutions. However, the interest rates will not be good, and some places may ask for security or large deposits to ensure that the company receives its money back. A better position would be a fair score of 601 to 660. Individuals with this rating will get credit more easily but still, have some issues with interest rates being high.

A good credit score (661–780) will ensure that a person is approved for credit and receive competitive interest rates. Vantage Score considers anything above 700 to be a great score and that number falls within a good rating. The best rating is excellent with scores between 781 and 850. These individuals will receive favorable interest rates and easily be approved for credit from some of the top lending companies.

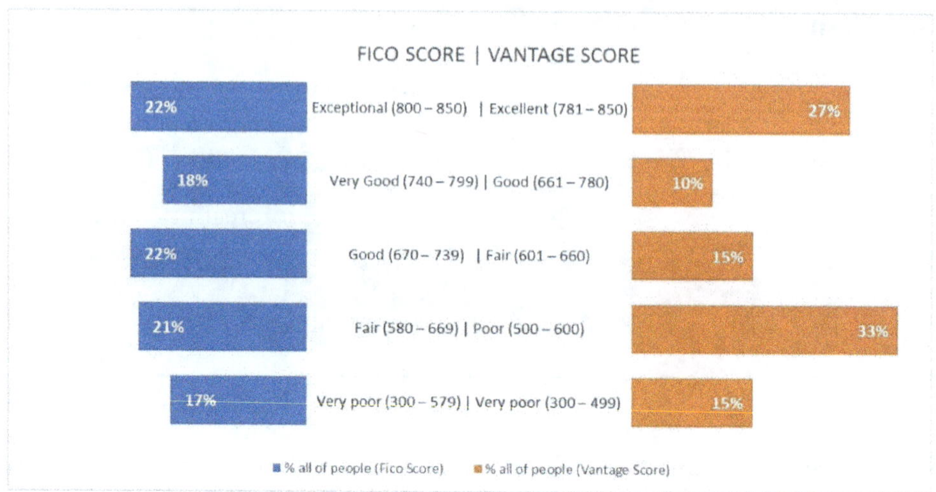

FICO SCORE | VANTAGE SCORE
22%
Exceptional (800 – 850) | Excellent (781 – 850)
27%
18%
Very Good (740 – 799) | Good (661 – 780)
10%
22%
Good (670 – 739) | Fair (601 – 660)
15%
21%
Fair (580 – 669) | Poor (500 – 600)
33%
17%
Very poor (300 – 579) | Very poor (300 – 499)
15%
% all of people (Fico Score)
% all of people (Vantage Score)

Chapter 2.

Understanding Credit Score

What Is a FICO Score?

The credit score structure was formulated by the Fair Isaac Corporation, also referred to as FICO. This credit score is utilized by financial institutions. There are other credit score models; however, the FICO score is the one that is most commonly used. Consumers can get and keep high credit scores by simply making sure their debt level remains low and they maintain an extended history of paying their bills as and when they are due.

In the FICO scoring formula, not all credit reports are scored equally.

Credit scores are weighted based on the particular "scorecard" that a person falls under.

For example, if the person has filed for bankruptcy, they may be scored using a special "bankruptcy" scorecard.

The credit score for a person under one scorecard may be affected differently by a negative event, like a late payment, than someone with the same event on a different scorecard. The scorecard you're on is determined by the most recent significant event in your credit history.

The first 10 scorecards go something like this:

Scorecards 1–5:

1. Those with public records, including judgments and bankruptcy, on their credit report.

2. For those with serious delinquencies other than bankruptcies (60, 90, 120 latest, collections, judgments, charge-offs repossessions, etc.).

3. Those with only 1 credit account (very thin files).

4. Those with only 2 credit accounts (thin files).

5. Those with only 3 credit accounts.

Scorecards 6–10 should not have any grave felonies (the definition of "serious" is unknown):

6. 0–2 years oldest account

7. 2–5 years oldest account

8. 5–12 years oldest account

9. 12–19 years oldest account

10. 19+ years oldest account

There is a total of 12 scorecards and they are subject to change as FICO (formerly Fair Isaac Corp) updates its scoring formula.

How Do You Check Your Credit Score?

It's a common misconception that you will automatically get your credit score when you get a copy of your credit report. This is not entirely the case. Credit reports usually do not include your credit score. It's also important to note that you do not have only one credit score. You will have at least three and more if you include the Vantage Score. They should be similar in range, but they will not usually be the same number because they are an estimate based on a series of calculations.

There are a few different ways you can try to access your credit scores. Look to our list for suggestions:

1. Check with your financial institutions. Many loaners such as credit card companies show your credit score as part of your account for free. If your creditors do not offer this, then you might be able to find the information on your online banking. Wells Fargo, for example, updates your credit score online once a month and shows how the number has changed and what is most influencing the score. It's as easy as logging in to your account and browsing the offered resources.

2. Just like you can order credit reports, you can also order a copy of your score from the three main credit bureaus, and FICO directly. This is a good option if your banking institution does not offer information or you are doing your yearly credit report check.

3. Some people choose to use credit score services, or free credit monitoring services to keep track of their credit score. Others offer greater resources and protection that charge, but there are many free ones. These are good options for those who are looking to keep track of their credit but don't want to spend the extra money for monitoring or to order directly from FICO.

What Information Is in a Credit Report?

Every credit bureau collects a lot of information about you, and all of that is included in your credit report. If someone wants to know about your credit usage in all these years, then one look at the credit report would reveal everything. The report has everything starting from whether you have cleared all your bills on time to the amount of debt that you might owe. The three credit bureaus, that is, Equifax, Experian, and Trans-union, are the ones that collect that information and compile them in the form of a report. All the information included in your report is collected from different sources (that is, lenders).

Whenever you want to apply for any type of loan or credit like student loans, credit cards, mortgage loans, and auto loans, every lender would want to have a look at your credit report. They will be granting you the credit only after they have evaluated your credit report, and everything seems fine. Your stats should match the terms set by them and if not, then you will not be getting your favorable rates.

The information that is present in your credit report is utilized in finding out your credit score. And all that information will be used by lenders to predict what your future behavior concerning credit is going to be.

Personal Information

This is the list of information that can be used in the future to identify you as a person. All of this information is not utilized to find your credit score. Some of the things that are included in this segment are your name, any misspellings that have been brought to light by creditors, aliases (if any), home addresses (past and current), Social Security Number, employers (past and current), and phone numbers.

Public Records

But any non-financial information or misdemeanors or arrests are not included here. It is solely meant for financial, legal actions, and if you have any public record in your credit report, then that is considered to be bad and you are probably not going to receive credits or loans.

Accounts

There are three categories to these accounts—closed, negative, and open. When you have been on good terms with the creditor, they will report the same. Your accounts will be in a good position. But sometimes you might not find certain account information because it was not reported by the creditors.

Some of the negative things that can be included are bankruptcies, late payments, or any type of account that has been forwarded to the collection or maybe charged off. If an account has been transferred or settled, then that might not have any bad impact on your score or report. It would definitely be something that any creditor would look more closely at.

Credit Inquiries

Usually, your credit report might have an inquiry up till two years from when it was made. Some things that are not mentioned in your credit report are your marital information, your education level, or even your bank balance. If a creditor has reported the name of your spouse, then that might be included in a report. But if you have had a divorce and you do not want the name of your spouse on the credit report, then you can proceed with disputing the information displayed on your credit report.

What Is a Good Credit Score? How Can I Improve My Credit Rating and Credit Score?

Your credit score is split into several levels but generally ranges from 300 to 850. The different credit rating levels are label as follows:

- 300 to 600: Bad Credit

- 600 to 649: Poor Credit

- 650 to 699: Fair Credit

- 700 to 749: Good Credit

- 750 + 850: Excellent Credit

The higher your credit score, the better. Better scores allow you to get credit easier, and with lower interest rates. Even when not getting credit, such as when you are renting an apartment, having a better credit rating builds trust with potential landlords.

The best thing that you can do to get your credit score up is to make payments on time. As soon as you start missing payments, your score will plummet. Delinquency can turn into a negative item that is much harder to remove. If you do miss payments, communicating and maintaining a good relationship with your creditor is key.

Chapter 3.

How to Manage your Credit Cards

How to Find Credit Cards with Guaranteed Approval?

What does true mean by promised approval? All credit cards come with some form of basic requirements before you are issued by a business. A key factor in those so-called secured credit cards is that the qualification requirements are usually minimal.

Milestone Master card – Less Than Perfect Credit Considered

The Milestone MasterCard provides a fast and easy application process and the use of all types of credit is encouraged. The card does not require a security deposit and is very welcoming to vulnerable creditors.

The Milestone Card may be used anywhere Visa is approved, according to the credit available.

Total Visa Card

The Full Visa Card is another card that does not need a security deposit and provides all the perks of a Visa full-service card. The card allows borrowers to have a current checking account, and a one-time service fee is charged. The lines of credit available are based on your actual credit score and credit worthiness.

How to Use a Credit Card Responsibly?

- Try not to use more than 30% of your credit card's limit.
- Make sure to always make payments on time. Even if it is the minimum payment!
- If you have the means, do your best to try and pay off your credit card balance in full each statement (this is not really all that realistic, I certainly couldn't do this in the past. But if you can, do so!)

How to Find Right Credit Card for You?

There is no one-size-fits-all credit card. Depending on your age and profession you will find certain credit cards more advantageous for your specific needs.

Credit Cards to Get a Balance Transfer

Even as credit cards include capacity accounts, stability switches. A credit card is one, which provides a low fee. If you happen to keep money, there is a stability switch a great way to go. The reduction in the promotional cost (and the more the promotional span), the larger the appealing card is. You may require a credit rating that is genuine to qualify.

Subprime Credit Rating Cards

Credit rating cards are among the credit rating card solutions. Those credit rating cards have been aimed at, and such cards have expenses and hobby prices. As acceptance is short for people who have an awful credit rating, the terms are hard.

Student Credit Cards

Student Credit Rating cards are those specifically made for those teens who have credit rating documents. Student credit rating cards may come, such as a cost or wages on balance transfers. College students commonly must be registered at a licensed 4-year university to become approved to get a student loan scorecard.

Restricted Cause Cards

Utilize motive Credit cards that are restricted can be handiest at locations. Rationale cards function using a fee and fund cost as credit rating cards. Gas credit rating cards and store credit rating cards are cases of motive credit scorecards that are restricted.

Secured Credit Rating Cards

Secured credit cards are an alternative rating repute. Cards call for a protection deposit to be set on the card. It might be additional in some instances—combined with a default, although the credit rating limitation on a credit rating card is equal to the amount of the deposit left on the card. It is worth noting that you predicted to create payments on your credit card balance.

How to Get an Installment Loan While Still in Bankruptcy

If you just filed for bankruptcy last week, you will have a very tough time quickly re-establishing credit. If some time has passed, you have a good shot at getting started though. It may be that a little more time is required before you can qualify for new credit lines. Even a relatively small mistake like maxing out a credit card or missing a utility bill can harm your credit score. Some might try to repair their credit from transactions they didn't think would harm their credit like closing an old account or even applying for a new loan.

Then there might be some who are trying to repair their credit after a major transgression like the declaration of bankruptcy. According to the reasons that have harmed your credit score, the time taken for repair will differ. This isn't a precise estimate and is only used as examples for your understanding. The recovery period will depend on several factors, along with the existing information on your credit report. If you have a long-standing credit history of timely payments, it is easier to repair any damage.

If your credit history is riddled with defaulting on payments, then it will take longer to fix any damage. Apart from this, your existing score matters too. Applicants that have either no credit or bad credit scores are seen to be high-risk borrowers, and that results in them having a decreased chance of being approved for a credit card or loan. Conversely, individuals with good credit scores are seen to be low-risk borrowers, and this increases the likelihood of them getting their applications approved. Credit scores by themselves do not control whether your loan request is approved or not. They are simply numbers created from a credit report. Lenders use them as a tool. Standards are set for what credit scores are acceptable, and the final decision is made. It does take a bit of time, but if you develop your credit well, that can make your credit scores improve and increase your chances of getting approval.

How to Get Lender to Remove a Lot of Days Late?

If you are currently behind on payments, ask the creditor if you can negotiate for a lower settlement amount, which includes their removing the late payments from your credit record after you have settled your debt. If they still want the full amount, then you may need to catch up before you can do anything else. If you cannot pay back your late payments, ask the creditor if you can work out a new payment plan that includes removal of the late payment information after you finish making a set number of payments, such as the first twelve monthly payments for the next year.

If they still want the full amount first, then you will have to get up to date on the amount owed. Once you are up to date with your payments, you can contact the creditor and plead your case to remove the negative late payment information. If you have a long-term relationship with them, let them know.

How to Get Credit Card Offers?

A clear majority of lenders don't have offers that are clearly defined upfront, instead, they have a general loan package that can be tweaked based on the situation individuals who come to them find themselves in. It becomes apparent why it is so important to seek out multiple offers before deciding.

To maximize this strategy, you are going to want to make a list of the features you are absolutely going to need to be happy with a given loan and then call each lender you have already talked to and go down the list point by point. If you come across a lender who has an approach that appeals to you, let the other lenders know about it and see what they can do to either match or beat it. They know they are in a competitive business and if you are willing to force their hand, they will show you just how much they want your business.

Pre-approved offers: If you have not opted out of the system, and your credit isn't terrible, then putting in an application with one lender will likely trigger a barrage of competing offers from other lenders as creditors will happily provide your information to anyone and everyone interested in selling you on their services.

While this can be annoying in some cases, if you are looking for the best lender possible then it could be just what you need to pit several lenders against one another. Pre-screened offers can make it easier for you to compare relative costs or special offers, as long as you do your due diligence with each and ensure that you aren't being hornswoggled by smoke and mirrors.

Ensure you have a loan estimate document: The loan estimate document was created by the Consumer Financial Protection Bureau to make it easier for borrowers to compare the various costs associated with individual loans and lenders. Its job is to standardize and simplify the way that lenders expose their fees so that you aren't comparing apples to oranges. The loan estimate document can be downloaded from ConsumerFinance.gov.

When and How to Open or Close a Credit Card

A major factor that plays into determining whether opening credit card accounts will be favorable to you or not is the credit utilization ratio. It is prudent to ensure that your credit utilization ratio is as low as possible.

Essentially, you must make sure that you are using too much credit. You might be tempted to close certain credit card accounts, especially if you have managed to pay off all your credit card dues. However, don't do this.

Don't allow the temptation to increase your spending to get a hold of you. Your credit utilization ratio can increase when you close an account. So, if you don't trust yourself with a credit card, you can store it away for safekeeping or keep it out of your reach.

A Technique for Paying Off Your Credit Card Debt

If all your accounts have a similar interest rate, the Snowball Method might be a better option, but if you have one or two cards with a scandalously high-interest rate, the Avalanche Method might be the right solution. It should be noted that both methods require that you have enough money to pay more than the minimum on your credit cards.

Avalanche Method

Using this method, people use the extra money they get each month to pay off the debt at the highest interest rate, with all minimum payments remaining. By eliminating higher interest payments faster, you'll pay less interest over the next few months until the total debt is paid off. Once you have paid off your first high-interest debt, find the next highest interest rate and repeat the process. Pay over the minimum amount as much as you can, so you can get out of debt faster.

Snowball Method

By following this method, people instead of focusing on the highest debt should first focus on paying off the card with the lowest debt until they reach the largest regardless of the interest rate. Then you work your way so you can pay the most you owe. Paying debts with the lowest amounts first, you pay off those smaller payments quickly and have fewer bills to worry about. Finally, you should continue to pay the bills with the lowest balances until you have no debt left.

Chapter 4.

Ways to Make and Save More Money with a High Credit Score

How to Use a Credit Card to Make Money and Earn Extra Cash

As you have all heard by now, you should maintain all your payments and keep low balances and you will live happily ever after. Yes, this is true, and you will get all that you deserve with a good foundation of credit like pre-approvals, more credit card solicitations than you actually want, and automatic credit line increases on your current credit card accounts, but that is not all. Once you get to this point, most so-called credit experts will stop giving you the advice that will take your credit to the next level. You have to be aware that with higher credit card limits and access to cash, you will be tempted in more ways than one and this could possibly be dangerous to the immature and undisciplined individual.

Primary Tradelines Vs. Authorized User Tradelines

When you think of boosting your credit score, the keyword in this process will be trade lines. During the process of building or rebuilding your credit, you applied for starter credit cards or maybe even a secured credit card or two. The credit cards or accounts you obtained during the building process are very critical to your success in developing a solid credit file. You can't have good credit without having positive reporting trade lines, especially revolving credit lines such as credit cards. Any account that you got approved for on your own is considered a Primary Account, you are the primary account holder and you hold all responsibilities for that account. Authorized User Tradelines exist only when a primary account holder adds a person to their credit card account.

Most major credit card companies allow any primary account holder to add up to 5 authorized users to their credit card account regardless of the credit limit. With this action, the account holder can control and designate how much access each authorized user can have or how long they choose to keep them on the account. Each time the creditor updates any activity related to the account with the credit bureaus for the primary account holder, they will report the exact same information for the authorized users of that account regardless of their responsibility for the account; including any late payments, balances, and even credit line increases. The age of the account will also be reported as a benefit to the authorized user. The backdated payment activity is the most beneficial feature of being added as an AU, the authorized user adopts the years' worth of positive payments, if you get added to a credit card account as an authorized user that is 10 years, your credit reports will reflect that you have made on-time payments for this account for 10 years, even if you were just recently added to the account. Beware, this tactic can backfire if the primary account holder has missed payments or normally carries balances higher than 30%, the authorized users will also pay the price of the negative information.

AU Tradelines

A primary credit card account is more favorable than an Authorized User Account as some computer systems and underwriters take into consideration the illusion that authorized user accounts can have when the FICO score is being generated. AU accounts can still be a very dangerous weapon for you to use, lenders have caught on to this technique as people would take a totally naked credit file, add 3 or 4 authorized user tradelines to the file, then apply for funding with the newly accumulated 700 plus credit scores. Understand that AU tradelines are still very effective, but you have to do a little more work to blend them into your credit boosting strategies. With the help of authorized user tradelines, it is very easy to get a "useless" 700–800 credit score that you will have a hard time getting the approvals for, even getting approved for the most basic cards can be difficult. It is very important to build your credit out the proper way to avoid a thin credit file with a high FICO score, you will be very disappointed as you rake up inquiries just to keep getting denied. Therefore, building a foundation is very important and you should not skip the starter credit cards.

Ideally, you will want a fresh credit file with no negatives reporting, which should have been your goal during the repair process. Once you finished your credit repair or if you are just beginning to build your credit for the first time, you will need to get approved for at least 2–3 primary tradelines to start with, I recommend you let those primary trade lines age for at least 4–5 months before applying for anything else. Once you have maintained 2–3 primary accounts, you can add two authorized user tradelines with some age and decent credit limits. With each AU tradeline being 5 years or older in age, and with limits of at least $10,000, you will be in a good position to secure your next level of primary accounts. You want to get away from those level 1 starter credit cards with small limits of $500–$1,000 and get to the point where all approvals will be levels 3 and 4 with $5,000 to $10,000 limits and above, this will be considered your first round of primary accounts. This is the proper position for a nice build-out of your credit file; I would suggest you obtain 2 or 3 approvals on this round at those limits. Every credit card you apply for now should be a credit card from a major issuer, American Express, Capital One, Discover, Citi bank,

Chase, or Credit Unions as they are more generous with approvals and credit limits.

The older the accounts, the better they are for everyone, as your primary credit accounts are aging, you should be learning. You can get in a position to help your family build credit or start your own community of credit for investment purposes without having to ask others for help. How powerful can you be when your whole family has perfect credit?

Typically, unless you get added as an authorized user from a family member or a friend, people will want to charge you, as the strategy of piggybacking on other people's positive credit accounts has become well known. It's standard for people to pay to be added to positive aged trade lines, companies exist and thrive on brokering these positive accounts to clients who need a boost in credit for funding purposes. This practice is 100% legal. The primary account holder can add authorized users by simply calling their credit card companies.

Find Out the Ways to Make and Save Money

Handling Addiction to Overspending

Overspending for them isn't the problem, but a consequence of the actual problems that can range from a desire to escape negative feelings or stressful situations to the urge to fill a gaping void left by unmet needs.

Let's look at the first psychological trigger for shopaholics: the desire to escape negative feelings. This trigger is prevalent in several cases of addiction. An impulsive buyer overspends for the same reason a chronic alcoholic cannot stop or doesn't want to stop after having a few bottles: to drown out the noise from the world. In other words, to escape an unpleasant reality and find momentary happiness.

For a shopaholic, the path to this addiction can be very innocuous. It could easily have started as a lady's friends coming around to take her shopping after she suffered a nasty breakup. She succumbs and then discovers. Her new acquisitions weren't going to reject her as her boyfriend did; they are hers forever. So, she goes home feeling much better. She soon discovers that her mind keeps digging up memories of her experience at the mall, and she subscribes to that therapy whenever she feels bad. Soon, all she can think of is burying her worries beneath several shopping sprees.

Several feelings addicts seek to escape from include depression, pain from the loss of a loved one, family crisis, and many others.

For some others, shopping can serve as plugs to clog voids created by unmet needs. Consider the case of a neglected trophy wife. She probably finds joy in hanging out with friends but discovers that the joy doubles when she's out throwing her husband's money around. The things she acquires, the people she's able to connect with because of her "generosity" are all emotional void fillers.

We've taken this short trip through the mind of an average shopaholic so that you can see that the problem cannot be solved by simply taking their credit cards away, I mean, are you saying they would never have access to them again? This beast needs to be taken down from below, from its roots, permanently.

Winning the Battle Against Shopping Addiction

Having established that addiction to shopping, which leads to overspending, is caused by the same root triggers of other forms of addiction, it is logical to conclude that the same methods used in dealing with these forms of addiction should prove effective in handling overspending. That aside, it is widely known that the predominant and most effective method of treating addiction is therapy.

The age of the account will also be reported as a benefit to the authorized user, even if you were just recently added to the account. Beware, this tactic can backfire if the primary account holder normally carries balances higher than 30%, the authorized users will also pay the price of the negative information.

With reports suggesting that between 5% and 9% of Americans have compulsive shopping disorders, finding help as a compulsive or impulsive spender isn't difficult at all. Addiction counselors are on the ground, and a good number of therapeutic interventions are being applied in helping addicts, including cognitive-behavioral therapy (CBT) and the 12-step program.

Cognitive-behavioral therapy looks to hijack the power of overspending by helping the addict challenge delusional beliefs, which are widely regarded as building blocks for the triggers of compulsive spending. Thoughts are believed to be sponsors of emotions and behaviors. CBT uses this assertion to attempt to assist addicts in influencing their feelings about shopping and remodeling their shopping behaviors by first reshaping their thoughts about the activity and getting their minds in the right place. This has been a very successful intervention program in treating many addictive behaviors.

While cognitive-behavioral therapy is majorly characterized by a single patient interacting with a trained therapist at regular intervals, group cognitive therapy is a more effective treatment for shopping addiction. This is perhaps due to the additional benefits that accompany being in a group of people battling the same problem. Addicts find themselves in a community of people who understand what they are faced with and can relate with them without being judgmental. Thoughts and struggles are shared freely, and burdens are borne communally. This helps a great deal in speeding up the healing process.

Plausible measures for putting your spending under control:

- Take someone with you when you shop.

- Put your credit cards out of your reach.

- Unsubscribe from retailer emails.

- Don't hang out around malls and retail stores.

- Use automated savings systems or apps.

Chapter 5.

Tips and Tricks to Raise Your Credit Score and Get 730+ Point

It is quite understandable that a person's creditworthiness can only be determined by the numbers he added to his name in this age of numbers game. A prospective loan applicant's proposal must be rejected if it has not yet reached a respectable base number of 700. A person's total loan count reflects the applicant's ability to disburse the prospective lender if the proposal is accepted. The number of loans usually varies between 340 and 850. The applicant's lack of respectable creditworthiness may be the reason why an application is rejected or, even if accepted, must increase an interest rate that would make it above the average to compensate the creditor in question. Some people find it uncomfortable not to have serious credit because they are unable to pay their bills and debts in full.

The lack of creditworthiness forces some to prepare for the worst by purchasing Master or Visa cards and credit cards for department stores only based on their payslips. Keep the appropriate records of your electricity bills before paying them all, as well as the invoices of all items that were intentionally purchased on credit to obtain a significant number. By overcoming all impulses for conspicuous consumption and instantly repaying bills of essential items, people in the United States are planning their financial operations to get good credit because they understand the importance of good credit that will not be compromised.

An impressive credit score can be achieved not only by planning transactions that add valuable points to the score but also by avoiding purchases where points are deducted to neutralize the advantage. It is often inconvenient for people to raise funds when they are unable to increase the monthly payment schedule, knowing that they cannot withstand the pressure, the eventuality of which at a reasonably decent number 1 score would influence the favorable terms. To keep the score reasonably decent, the borrower is forced to seek a new loan that goes beyond official records and that a lender can accept by charging a higher interest rate. Too many credit cards mean too many small balances, which means too many irrelevant allocations of the debtor's credit-related activities, which cannot contribute to the accumulation/improvement. Therefore, it is advisable to cancel the cards and keep only two cards that have the longest history and the lowest interest rate. Before three years of credit history, you shouldn't make the usual mistake of opening a new account if there is no obligation. You should get into the habit of turning credit updating on and off, especially when you approach 700.

Raise Your Credit Score

Correcting all errors in your credit report should be effective by referring the error with support to the agency in the matter, the documents that it can control and act.

The unlikely magic number of the loan, e.g. H. 700 or higher, can be achieved by increasing efforts to maintain it. Once there, you can take advantage of loans at reduced interest rates, which can differ, for example, for tuition fees for renovating a house and buying houses or cars.

One should be competent enough to use creditworthiness to determine the possibility of a loan, which would surely save him a lot of time, energy, money, and perhaps embarrassment.

Next on the list is to find ways that you can limit the liability that you are dealing with. When you go to co-sign a loan, remember that this may seem like a nice thing to do, but you are really taking on a risk for another person. If you do this for someone who is not able to manage their debt all that well, it is going to negatively affect your score because you will be responsible for that debt as well. If you want to make sure that you can get a credit score that is 800+, and maintain that, then it is a good idea to avoid co-signing at all. In addition to this one, you should make sure that your liability is limited in other ways as well. You should always report your cards that have been lost or stolen right away. If you don't do this, then it is likely that you will be liable for any of the purchases that are not authorized at the time. And if you are not able to afford those purchases, then your score is going to be the thing that suffers here.

And finally, we need to make sure that we are restricting the hard inquiries that happen to our report. Whether it is you or another agency or institution who is pulling out the credit report and asking for a copy of it, you are dealing with an inquiry. A soft inquiry can happen on occasion as well, and it is generally not going to be enough to make any changes to your credit. This soft inquiry is going to happen when one of the following occurs:

1. You go through and do a check on your own credit report.

2. You give an employer you may work with in the future permission to go through and check your credit.

3. You have the financial institutions that you do business with go through and check your credit.

4. You get a credit card offer that has been preapproved, and that specific company goes through and checks your credit.

While the soft inquiry is not going to do all that much to our credit scores, we do need to be careful about the hard inquiry. This is going to be the one that can affect your credit score. It is when a company is going to pull up your credit report after you apply for a product like a credit card or a mortgage. You want to make sure that you can limit the hard inquiries as much as possible to get the best results with this.

Will Debt Consolidation Hurt My Score in a Negative Way?

Simply put, this means putting all your debts into one account, meaning you will owe money only to one credit institution and pay them only once a month (or bi-weekly or weekly depending on what you negotiate).

In the process, your new creditor will pay off your current creditors, meaning you now owe all your debt to this one new creditor.

The idea behind this is that your new interest rate will be lower than the combined interest rate you had before, meaning you can pay off your debt quicker because more of your money is going towards paying off your capital instead of going straight into interest.

It also makes things much simpler and less stressful for you, since having just one payment to worry about is much less to think about and easier to budget than several throughout the month.

That will give you the lowest interest rate. However, depending on where you are in time with your mortgage term, it can come with some very high fees that may represent more than any interest saved.

Remortgaging might also not provide you with enough cash to pay off all your other debts. So, here we will look at the process of debt consolidation for any remaining debts and how to decide the best plan of attack for your situation.

Other Considerations for Debt Consolidation

Whilst finding the lowest interest rate is the most important thing here, there are a few other considerations that are very important when negotiating to consolidate your debts:

1. Sometimes financial institutions will only allow you to have a lower rate when it is combined with a longer repayment period. This means that even though you are paying less in

interest every month, you will pay more in the long term than you would do before you consolidated. This is because you are paying it off over a longer period than you would do before. So, even though your monthly payments are lower, you are in fact paying more in the long term, which really defies the point of consolidating in the first place. This really buys you some wiggle room financially in the short term but is really hurting you more in the long term.

2. Sometimes financial institutions will put restrictions on how much and how often you can pay off extra amounts. This can be really frustrating as occasionally you may come into some extra cash (maybe an annual bonus, a small inheritance, or some extra overtime). When you are committed to paying off your debt as quickly as possible, the obvious (and sensible) thing to do is put the extra money into paying off your debt. However, many people come unstuck as they didn't consider this when signing with their debt consolidator. Remember, the financial institutions want you to pay it off over a longer period as possible to maximize their profit. They might be pretty sneaky with this, so always be clear with them about what you want and read the contract carefully. This is also important because if you don't have the option to pay off any lump sum along the course of your repayment schedule, it means you are effectively forced to pay off a slightly lower amount than you think you can afford each month. After all, there are always unexpected life events that you can't budget

for, especially if you are paying it off over many years. You always need some wiggle room throughout the duration of your debt repayment. Situations always change in unexpected ways.

Chapter 6.

Most Common Errors Found in Credit Reports and How to Avoid Them

According to the federal trade commission, 1 in 5 Americans has a mistake on their credit report. In other words, approximately 40 million Americans have an error on their credit report; this number is not only astounding but is very revealing. Therefore, a lot of people are being denied credit based on inaccurate information found on their credit files. Also, some people are paying high-interest rates based on errors that were found in their credit reports.

Three common mistakes that cause errors on credit reports:

- Sometimes people inadvertently provide the wrong social security number when applying for credit.
- People sometimes make a mistake when they enter your information on a credit application.

- An account that belongs to John Smith Sr. sometimes will get reported as owned by John Smith Jr.

Note that there could be various mistakes in each of the three credit reports. It is not uncommon to have positive coverage of an account on one article, but poor reports on another.

Here are others of the most common credit report errors:

- Listed wrong names, emails, or phone numbers.

- Data that refers to another of the same name.

- Duplicate details, whether positive or negative, about the same account.

- Records have negative, apparently positive information.

- Balances on accounts payable are still on view.

- Delinquent payment reports that were never billed in due time.

- This indicates wrong credit limits.

- Claims included in the insolvency which is still due.

- Incorrect activity dates.

- Past-due payments not payable.

- Court records that are falsely connected with you, such as convictions and bankruptcy.

- Tax liens, not yours.

- Unprecedented foreclosures.

- Incorrect names.

- Wrong address.

- Wrong social security number.

- Accounts not belonging to you.

- Accounts with the incorrect credit limit.

- Open accounts being reported as closed.

- Closed accounts being reported as open.

- Account incorrectly reported as being late.

- Out-dated information.

- The mixture of the two different credit reports.

- Identity theft.

- An account listed twice.

- Incorrect phone number.

- Authorized user listed as the owner of an account.

- Ex-spouse information listed on the credit report.

- Incorrect account status.

How to Prevent Common Errors on Your Credit Report?

It can be very disheartening to discover that you might have errors on your credit report, but taking steps to prevent errors from being placed on your credit report can help you to avoid a lot of unnecessary stress. Take extra caution to secure yourself against identity theft. You should consider setting up credit monitoring alerts to inform you whenever a recent update has been made to your credit report, act fast to correct any errors on your credit report, and double-check any information you provide to a creditor when you apply for credit. Many times, if you have had a long-term account with a creditor, you can contact them directly and explain the error being reported on your credit report.

Ask them to write you a letter with the email and correction. Also, ask them to contact every credit reporting agency that reports this incorrect entry to correct.

Once the creditor receives a copy of the letter, make a copy of it, and attach the letter to the letter of the dispute you send. Mail it to the agency for credit reporting and ask them to update their files. Once that is completed, you will be sent back a new credit report by the credit reporting agency.

Chapter 7.

Managing Debt

Your credit use rate or the aggregate sum of accessible debt utilized on your accounts (unsecured and secured) is the second biggest factor toward obtaining a solid credit score. Besides your verified debt, which is paid down according to a calendar and doesn't increase in the amount owed, we should concentrate here on uncollateralized debt, which is the costliest debt, and furthermore, the debt that is least demanding to gain out of power. In case you're overpowered with debt or have burrowed a huge gap from which you're uncertain how to begin moving out, my first advice is to unwind. There is absolutely no motivation to experience the ill effects of superfluous uneasiness or stress in light of debt. Losing rest and agonizing night and day over fortuitous debt won't assist you with receiving in return, so accept the way that you are in debt and start considering how and when you can receive in return.

Credit Card Debt Is the Costliest Debt

Credit card debt is the most choking-out debt of all, and the feeling of always digging and getting no placc is a feeling to which I can relate very well. Don't give it a chance to make you crazy. With an activity plan and being persevering not to overextend yourself, you can gradually arrive at a point where your credit card debt is neither bringing you nor your credit score down. While I'm not a specialist in credit card debt guiding.

I realize that in my circumstance, I had the option to toss little lumps of my compensation at this pile of debt — a few months in bigger pieces, others in littler pieces—until I had a little enough balance to clear out. While this segment intends to provide some practical tips on the most proficient method to manage your debt, if you believe you are absolutely up the creek without a paddle, or a significant life event, for example, joblessness, or a medicinal issue or anything that is preventing you from having the option to pay down any of your debt, at that point jumping to the following segment might be progressively appropriate for you.

Debt Management Tips

For those of you who are in the limbo period of, "Should I pay-down debt," or "Should I file bankruptcy," comprehend that there are two types of personal bankruptcy: the main, Bankruptcy, takes into consideration most or the entirety of your debts to be discharged or dropped. The second, known as Bankruptcy, plan your debt for repayment over some time. If you are thinking about both choices, at that point it is highly recommended that you search out somebody with mastery; for example, a bankruptcy trustee or lawyer. Sometimes everything necessary is a professional's advice and a helping hand to guide you correctly. If you are going to attempt to dig yourself out of debt without documenting personal bankruptcy or choosing your debts for not exactly the aggregate sum owed with your creditors, you have to have a plan.

What's the Best Approach to Deal with Huge Credit Card Debt?

There is no doubt that the interest on credit card debt can be an executioner. Many credit cards have interest rates of more than 20%. If you utilize Chris' Debt Repayment Calculator (at welker.ca) you can perceive the amount it will cost to pay off your credit cards with interest for more than five years. Perhaps the biggest error that people make when they are attempting to dig themselves out of debt all alone is making payments that simply spread the interest charges but aren't really lessening the head.

Chris Walker says that if you are battling to deal with your credit card debt and you need to pay back what you can bear, at that point the best alternative may be a consumer proposal for a repayment. By offering a consumer proposal, you can stop interest charges, prevent creditor collection activity, and settle your debt.

While documenting a consumer proposal briefly damages your credit rating, it is frequently the best approach for people dealing with huge credit card debt. Don't make the mistake of concentrating on your credit rating. While credit rating is important, improving your financial wellbeing is undeniably progressively important. You can generally modify your credit rating, yet If you don't have a plan to escape debt, you will continue to battle.

Know common
mistakes
and
avoid them

If You Need to Manage Your Credit Card APRs

In cases of medical or employment hardships, or some other setbacks in life, creditors will sometimes permit a decrease or freeze on additional fund charges to your existing debt. Everything necessary is calling to discover what they can do after disclosing to them your circumstance—it might be critical enough to accommodate their explanation codes or extraordinary programs. Creditors frequently save these for people who might not be able to make payments on time or the full amount of the average monthly payments owed, and the programs may keep going for set periods of six months to a year or more.

In return for enrolling in these programs, a few creditors may likewise stop your account preventing you from making additional buys and adding to your existing debt. Obviously, you won't realize what options you have until you call, so in case you're reluctant about grabbing the telephone, discover the time to call every one of your creditors and examine these options that could bring some truly necessary help. Ask if as to whether you can make a lesser monthly payment.

This would be your most solid option if you are still ready to manage a smidgen of a monthly payment, notwithstanding any plans for a DIY debt settlement. You'll be happy you called—anything to help diminish the amount of interest charged and APRs consistently. The goal here is to get what, assuming any, options you have, at managing or keeping your balances low. Twofold check that by enrolling yourself in any diminished APR or APR-freezing programs, creditors will continue reporting to the

CRAs that you are making timely payments. (Creditors can begin reporting harsh payments if a bill is 30 days overdue.)

Settling Your Own Debts

While personal debt settlement was to a great extent a totally unbelievable practice, as meager as five years ago, plenty of DIY debt pilgrims have now taken their accounts of the process to online media and web journals. More news and research on the subject, by and large, has additionally now put the process inside go after the individuals who wish to take the creditors head-on. Many have picked this course to be in all-out control of their settlement process as opposed to enlisting an outsider debt arbitrator to intercede. You can settle your debts all alone; anyway, you should be prepared and solid-willed. You'll need to suffer and confront creditors' and debt collectors' endeavors and strategies at getting you to pay up, which can be out and out forceful and smooth. Furthermore, you will be sorted out by managing and monitoring the results of each arranged account. People are procured by organizations to make debt collection their full-time exertion and are compensated accordingly, so don't overlook they are professionals at endeavoring to get anything they can out of any debtor.

Debt settlement is positively an option for any individual who basically can't make payments or who has fallen so behind that the subsequent stage would resort to bankruptcy. An outline of personal debt settlement includes:

1. Halting any payments on every uncollateralized debt that you can't pay. Right away.

2. Pausing and avoiding creditors as they attempt to chase you down to collect their outstanding payments. If they have your telephone number, it is alright getting another PDA saved for loved ones. The goal is to release the account until it gets so far financially past due that they will be desperate to settle with you before charging off the account.

3. Proposing a debt settlement for as meager as 20% of the amount you owe. This may require some intense arrangement and standing your ground.

4. Affirming everything in writing from the creditor regarding any debt settlement and payback terms. It is prudent to not fall for a reset of the process by sending in any cash until you have, in your grasp, the creditor's letter plotting the terms that are agreeable to you.

Once more, personal debt settlement isn't for everybody. Debt settlement will assuredly damage your credit when creditors and collection agencies continue reporting reprobate payments on your accounts.

You'll get a good deal on any charges you'd pay debt directing or combination organizations to consult for your sake. Likewise, you may have an easier time with creditors, since your creditors and collectors will realize they're dealing straightforwardly with you rather than an agent, who might be harder to work with. Creditors may go easier on you.

Chapter 8.

Identity Theft

Did you ever wonder if people are becoming the perpetrators of identity theft? Or maybe you have been and you're not sure how it happened. There are plenty of approaches used by hackers to get your personal information a hold.

Theft of identity is one form of fraud. It is defined as taking or claiming the identity of another person to use existing accounts, open new credit accounts, or receive other benefits for a fraudulent reason from their personal information. A person's credit cards are usually used for making purchases. Social Security cards and numbers were also taken to establish new credit in your name.

How Identity Theft Happens

Identity theft happens in a variety of ways; hackers obtain access to your personal information by removing it from your purse or wallet, impersonating an official representative, and accessing your identity through mail and computer technology. Here are some of the way's identity thieves get your personal data:

- ***Skimming****.* Occasionally, there may be a special storage device connected to the card reader while you swipe your credit card or debit card during a normal transaction. This system collects and stores up to several hundred numbers per credit card at a time. When you transfer the details to a computer, the identity thief will have access to your information without even realizing it.

- ***Hacking****.* Most identity thieves are also hackers. For businesses that have personal records for the place, they will use smart technology to hack into your personal computers or computer systems. Many banks were also victims of malware and all of their clients may have been victims of identity theft.

- ***Stealing mail****.* The e-mail provides credit card statements, tax information, bank statements, credit deals pre-approved, and even new checks. Thieves will rob from your mailbox right away and were even known to have mail sent to them. This confidential information is at their disposal and can help them rob your identities.

- ***Dumpster diving****.* Identity thieves also rummage through your personal garbage, something that often occurs in companies. Robbers search and locate bank account numbers, credit card numbers, financial statements, and other personal information through the trash.

- ***Employees of businesses****.* Identity thieves can sometimes steal personal records from businesses. This could be an employee's role-taking company documents from his or her own boss to gain access to confidential information. Many identity thieves at a business may conspire with an employee who can give them access to personal records. Therefore, workers receiving credit reports can violate their rights to that information.

- ***E-mails and phone calls.*** Identity hackers were known to impersonate your broker, trustee, or other company representatives by calling or giving you an e-mail. Do not do so if you receive a mysterious phone call or e-mail demanding your personal information to either check your account or to claim money. They most likely try to steal your credit card number, Social Security number, or other account numbers, whatever the scheme.

- ***Home theft.*** Many robbers are trying to break into your home not to steal your television or jewels, but to take your name. They will steal tax information, bank account numbers, Social Security numbers, number of credit card accounts, and any other personal information they might discover.

What to Do If You Are a Victim of Identity Theft

Have you ever seen this happen? You just received a collection notice in the mail for an account you didn't use or even know about, you received a credit card in the mail you never wanted or opened, or you were simply turned down for a loan or credit card due to a low FICO score with accounts that weren't even yours.

If there has been one of these cases, you are most likely a victim of identity theft.

You might feel robbed, betrayed, and left wondering how this might happen to you. Your credit scores were most likely impacted negatively. You may need a loan or credit, and this condition prohibits you from receiving it. To fix the damage that has already happened and to mitigate potential future harm, you need to take control and figure out what to do next.

Criminal laws regulate identity theft. According to the Identity Theft and Assumption Deterrence Act of 1998, it is a felony to "consciously pass or use, without legal authority, a means of identifying another person to commit, or aid or abetting, any criminal conduct that constitutes a breach of Federal law or that constitutes a crime under any State or local statute applicable."

The law is in place to provide offenders with a consolidated complaint process, as well as improve the criminal laws surrounding identity theft. If you're a victim of identity theft, prompt action is required. The law allows claimants to challenge unauthorized charges; however, some time-limits need to be followed.

- ***Notify the creditor.*** When you find unauthorized charges on your credit or debit card, then you were most likely a victim of identity theft. The good news is that the Equal Credit Billing Act limits any responsibility for unauthorized charges to $50. When you discover the unauthorized charges, you will have to write down your trustee, disputing the questionable payments.

  Write the letter of disagreement to the agency "Billing inquiries" of your creditor. Make sure you send the certified letter to your trustee and you know it's hitting you. Notify the creditor as soon as the unwanted payment is identified and make sure that your letter hits them within 60 days of the first bill revealing the mistake. Keep yourself a copy of the letter. Under the statute, the creditor must respond within 30 days of receiving the message, and the conflict must be settled within two billing cycles.

- *Notify your bank.* If your debit card has been stolen, you will report it to your bank within two working days. Under the Electronic Fund Transfer Act, you will only be held liable for $50 in unauthorized charges; however, you will be responsible for $500 of unauthorized charges if you report the unauthorized charges between three and 60 days. Unless you wait until 60 days later, you can lose all of the money stolen from your account. If your debit card has a Visa or MasterCard mark, both firms will limit your liabilities to $50 per card in unauthorized charges.

  It's better that you alert your suppliers and banks as soon as you can or your debit cards, credit cards, and even personal checks have been stolen if you detect fraudulent charges. The longer you wait to contact the lender, the greater the chance that some or all of the unauthorized charges will be placed on you.

- *Fraud alert.* If you've been a victim of identity theft, it's important to create a warning about fraud. If you call credit reporting agencies, you will have to choose between two different types of fraud alerts—the expanded warning and the original notice.

The expanded notice entitles you to receive two free credit reports from each credit reporting agency per year; however, for seven years, the fraud alert must stay on your register. The most common type of warning against fraud is the original alarm. This will live 90 days on your file and will send you one free credit report from each of the three reporting agencies.

You must have a police report and evidence of the theft or attempted fraud to create an extended warning. You may request that for your protection, only the last four digits of your Social Security number appear on your credit report. You may also cancel any warning about fraud at any time.

To set up a fraud alert for your own protection is in your best interest. This means the robber can't open credit in your name. You will notify the other credit reporting offices if you call one of the credit reporting agencies to set up the fraud alert.

Your credit report and credit score are important to you and your future earnings. Make sure you check them regularly to ensure you're not a victim of identity theft.

- ***Police report***. If you suspect that you are a victim of identity theft, it is in your best interests to lodge a police report. Some creditors may require that a police report be used as evidence of the incident. Many police stations hesitate to take a call on identity theft. Assure your submission is permanent. Make sure that you have a copy of the report for your history, because credit card companies and banks may need to see the report and search for unauthorized charges. Remember, make sure that you have the name and phone number of the prosecutor, in case the investors need to talk to him or her.

- ***Social Security Administration.*** If your Social Security card has been stolen or you know your Social Security number has been used to open new accounts, you will call the Department of Social Security. They will most of the time issue you a new Social Security number and card. To apply for a new Social Security number, you must provide evidence that someone using your account is still harming you. Your sex, U.S. residency, or legal immigration status, and name will need to be confirmed.

- ***Postal inspector.*** When you believe that your mail was robbed or sent to a different location, you were most likely a victim of identity theft in which a criminal rummaged through your mail or used a Change of Address form to give them your mail. Contact the postal inspector for documentation and prosecute this fraud.

- ***Department of Motor Vehicles.*** If your driver's license has been stolen, you need to contact your state agency that issued your license. Most of the time, you can locate their contact information by checking the Department of Motor Vehicles in your state online. They will cancel your license and give you instructions on how to get another license.

- Federal Trade Commission. You will report the crime to the Federal Trade Commission (FTC) if you've been a victim of identity theft. Call them at IDTHEFT (877), or at www.idtheft.gov.

Although the FTC does not prosecute identity theft, it exchanges concerns with local regulatory bodies that support the federal fight against identity theft.

Chapter 9.

How Credit System Works

In a nutshell, the entire credit system constitutes the credit bureaus, the creditors, and you. Creditors are the companies you access credit from while the credit bureaus collect credit data from past and current creditors and compile it into reports, which are modeled in the form of credit profiles for each credit consumer, after which they sell these reports to creditors so that they can make various decisions.

The creditors use the data they obtain from credit bureaus to determine how much they will charge you for borrowing and the number of penalties they should charge you for defaulting. Whenever a creditor needs credit profiles of people that have a certain credit score, they buy that information from the credit bureaus. This helps them to target their products and services since they will then send emails to those in that list enticing them to buy or use their products and services. It is believed that most of these companies go after those that have a low score.

This will allow them to have a chance at making a greater profit and pulling out as much money as possible from these people's pockets.

The credit system consists of three parties namely you, the creditors, and the credit bureaus.

If a creditor needs a report of credit consumers who have a specific credit score, they can then buy the credit profiles from the credit bureaus, thus making it easy to target products and services appropriately. They (creditors) will send you enticing information on offers that you should buy.

Subprime credit data is the best-selling for the different credit reporting agencies. Therefore, if you have a subprime credit rating, you are likely to be getting countless email solicitations for you to apply to different credit cards. The reasoning for this is straightforward. With a subprime credit rating, you are going to be charged more for accessing credit. This simply means that the lenders will make more money from you. If you have an excellent credit rating, you are low risk and lenders charge you less for accessing credit, which means that they make less money when they advance your credit. In other terms, lenders will want to prey on you if you have bad credit because they are sure that they will make more money in the end. Even if you are to default, you are likely to have paid more money than someone who has good credit!

Subprime data is such a hot selling product that the credit reporting agencies charge more for it; it is in high demand! This can be translated to mean that the creditors and credit bureaus don't care about you having good credit. In any case, if your credit rating is bad, they will charge you more! Do you know that over 90% of credit reports have been proven to have inaccurate, unverifiable, and erroneous entries?

Get to Know
Credit System

Well, now you know why your credit score is always becoming bad, even with all your effort. These companies are in it for profit. They will even overlook when erroneous entries are posted in your report. In any case, they have convinced us to think that the reports are the gospel truth when they are nowhere close to that. So, in simple terms, these two players in the credit system can only be compelled by the law to put things in order. They have no interest in you having perfect credit because they all make more money if you have bad credit.

If you are in this group of credit consumers, you will get the most enticing offers and email solicitations to apply for credit cards. The reason is simple, as mentioned when your credit score isn't so good, the creditors will charge more for advancing your credit, which means that they make more money. In financial terms, creditors address their exposure to credit risk by charging more for credit. If you can pay the right amount on time, this will cause them to lose out on a substantial amount of profit. They will not be satisfied with what they receive and will want more out of their customers. They might not directly refuse you credit, but they will not be particularly interested in giving you money. They will be waiting for someone with bad credit to walk in. When you have poor credit, you might be paying up to three times what you would pay were you to have a perfect credit score.

So, the companies will expressly go after those that have a bad score and will put in all possible effort to trap them. As you can see, creditors will be inclined to prey on those with sub-prime credit scores for the simple reason that they will make more money from them even if they were to default, as they will have already made money! So, there is a lot of planning that they do just to fill up their pockets.

It should not surprise you that these companies work hand in hand. It takes effort from both ends for their schemes to work and they will ensure that they are on the same page. They will come up with plans that will benefit both and cause each to make a large profit at the expense of the customer. Imagine trying to cheat millions of customers yearly, it is a Herculean task and will require the company to be as prepared as possible to pull it off with ease. For this reason, they will join hands and make sure each one cuts into the profit.

Apart from these two, there will be some third parties who will work to help these credit companies. These can be outsourced companies or independent ones looking to hook up with the credit companies and trying to make money for themselves. These will have the exclusive job of looking for people that have not checked their records for some time and determine to get them on board. They will put in a lot of effort to catch these people's fancy and once they trap them, they will direct them to the credit company and get them to pay for their services.

To prove that your bad credit history records are a best seller for credit reporting agencies, do you know that they will even charge more to credit providers to access such information? That's right, they will pay up a little more just to find those that have bad credit and start bombarding them with emails that ask them to apply for credit at their place. This means that none of these parties has any specific interest to have the information accurately reported in your credit report.

Do you know that only a small percentage of people file disputes for such items despite over 90% of credit reports have been found to have erroneous, unverifiable, and inaccurate entries? Many will not wish to go through the pain of proving they are right. This allows the companies to have a long leash and they will not back away from exploiting these people.

If you have a subprime credit rating, you are likely to be getting countless email solicitations for you to apply to different credit cards. With a subprime credit rating, you are going to be charged more for accessing credit, because the lenders will make more money from you. In other words, lenders will want to prey on you if you have bad credit because they are sure that they will make more money in the end.

The companies have several good field days owing to such ignorance on the part of the customers.

The credit companies will be determined to report your bad credit and this means that some of them will even let such entries be included in your credit report for the simple reason that very few of us have the guts to challenge entries in the credit report, even if they are incorrect, unverifiable and erroneous. They will know who exactly will not challenge it just by looking at your credit history. They will not have an interest in catering to those that might take up a dispute. They will employ people to look especially for those customers who have a bad score and those who look most likely to remain mum about errors in their reports.

The two other players in the credit system (the creditors and the credit reporting agencies) are in it to make the most money from you directly or indirectly, so counting on them to help you make things right should be out of the question.

The more screwed up your credit score is, the more money there is to be made by the credit reporting agencies and the creditors. That is, the lower the score, the better their prospects to charge you a bomb.

So, when you file a dispute, the creditors and the credit reporting agencies will only update the data, not because they have any interest in your welfare, but because they don't have an option given to them and they are under a legal obligation to act under the law. They will not expressly pursue your cause and, in fact, despite your efforts to fix your bad score, they will try and remain ignorant of it and make things worse for you. They will go to any lengths just to make sure that you have no chance of fixing your score despite it is not your fault.

This is the exact reason why there are hundreds, probably thousands, of people who despise credit card companies. They will not stop at anything and fall to absolute lows just to make a few extra dollars. Many of these companies will have a bad reputation and yet find easy prey for themselves.

They will know how exactly they can target the customers and get them to subscribe to their card. Once the person is trapped, they will not stop until they fulfill their desire to make as much money as possible. The poor customer will be trapped and will have to surrender to the demands of the vicious company.

Every day, there are hundreds of innocent customers who fall for this trick and do not put in the effort to check their credit reports. But it is important for every person to thoroughly go through their report and look for any erroneous and wrong entries that may be causing them their low scores.

Now that you understand that only you are on your side on matters about the accuracy of the credit report, how do you know how your credit score affects your ability to borrow? It is apparent that your score is the most vital element in your report and something that needs to be investigated carefully. But what is this score and what are its parameters? How do you know that your score is good, average, or bad?

Of course, the report doesn't state that a certain amount is bad, so understanding what benchmarks the lenders are going to use in categorizing you as good (perfect), average (sub-prime), and bad will be very helpful so that you know what to expect when you see that number on your credit report.

Chapter 10.

Credit Scoring Myth

For a large portion of credit scoring's history, by far, most of the people engaged with loaning decisions pretty much needed to think about what hurt or helped a score. Makers of scoring formulas would not like to uncover much about how the models functioned, for dread that contenders would take their thoughts or that consumers would understand how to beat the framework.

Luckily, today we discover much increasingly about credit scoring—however, not every person has stayed aware of the latest knowledge.

Mortgage intermediaries, loan officials, credit agency agents, credit guides, and the media, among others, continue to spread outdated and out and out bogus information.

Following up on their terrible guidance can put your score and your accounts at critical risk.

Here are probably the most widely recognized fantasies.

Let's Debunk
Some Myth

Myth 1: Closing Credit Accounts Will Help Your Score

This one sounds sensible, particularly when a mortgage merchant discloses to you that lenders are suspicious of people who have heaps of unused credit accessible to them. What's you, all things considered, from hurrying out and charging up a tempest?

Obviously, looking at the situation objectively, what's shielded you from piling on huge balances before now? If you've been responsible with credit before, you're probably going to continue to be responsible later.

That is the essential standard behind credit scoring: Its rewards practices that show moderate, responsible utilization of credit after some time, because those propensities are probably going to continue.

The score likewise rebuffs conduct that is not all that responsible, for example, applying for a lot of credit you don't require.

Numerous people with high credit scores locate that one of only a handful hardly any detriments for them is the number of credit accounts recorded on their reports. At the point when they go to get their credit scores, they're informed that one reason their score isn't considerably higher is that they have "too many open accounts."

Many mistakenly expect they can "fix" this issue by closing accounts. In any case, after you've opened the accounts, you've done the damage. You can't fix it by closing the account. However, you can make things more awful.

Myth 2: You Can Increase Your Score by Asking Your Credit Card Company to Lower Your Limits

This one is a minor departure from the possibility that decreasing your accessible credit in one way or another enables your score by making you seem less risky to lenders. Little by little, it's missing the goal. Narrowing the difference between the credit you use and the credit you have accessible to you can negatively affect your score.

It doesn't make a difference that you requested the decrease; the FICO formula doesn't recognize lower limits that you mentioned and lower limits forced by a creditor.

All it sees is less difference between your balances and your limits, and that is not good. If so, you need to enable your score to handle the issue from the opposite end: by paying down your debt. Expanding the gap between your balance and your credit limit positively affects your score.

Myth 3: You Need to Pay Interest to Obtain a Good Credit Score

This is the precise inverse of the past myth, and it's similarly misinformed. You don't need to carry a balance on your credit cards and pay interest to have a good score. As you've perused a few times as of now, your credit reports—and subsequently the FICO formula—make no differentiation between balances you carry month to month and balances that you pay off.

Savvy consumers don't carry credit card balances under any circumstances, and not improve their scores. Presently, the facts confirm that to get the highest FICO scores, you must have both revolving accounts, for example, credit cards, and installment loans, for example, a mortgage or car loan. What's more, except for those 0% rates used to drive auto deals after Sept. 11, most installment loans require paying interest.

Yet, here's a news streak: You don't have to have the highest score to get good credit. Any score more than 720 or so will get you the best rates and terms with numerous lenders. A few, particularly auto and home value lenders, save their best bargains for those with scores of more than 760. You don't just have an 850, or even 800 scores, to get incredible arrangements. In case you're attempting to improve a fair score, a little and reasonable installment loan can help—if you can get affirmed for it and pay it off on time. However, one way or another, there's no motivation to stray into the red and pay interest.

Myth 4: Your Closed Accounts Should Indicate "Closed by Consumer," Or They Will Hurt Your Score

The hypothesis behind this myth is that lenders will see a closed account on your credit report and, if not educated generally, will accept that a nauseated creditor cut you off because you botched in one way or another. Obviously, as you most likely are aware at this point, numerous lenders never observe your real report.

They're simply taking a gander at your credit score, which couldn't care less who closed a credit card. Fair Isaac figures that if a lender closes your account, it's either for dormancy or because you defaulted. If you default, that will be sufficiently archived in the account's history. If it makes you feel better to contact the bureaus and guarantee that accounts you closed are recorded as "closed by consumer," by all methods do as such. However, it won't make any distinction to your credit score.

Myth 5: Credit Counseling Is Way Worse Than Bankruptcy

Sometimes this is expressed as "credit advising is as awful as bankruptcy" or "credit directing is as terrible as a bankruptcy." None of these statements is valid. A bankruptcy recording is the single most noticeably terrible thing you can do to your credit score.

On the other hand, the current FICO formula totally ignores any reference to credit guiding that may be on your credit report. Credit guiding is treated as an impartial factor, neither aiding nor hurting your score. Credit guides, if you're inexperienced with the term, have practical experience in arranging lower interest rates and also working out payment plans for debtors that may in one way or another file for bankruptcy.

Although credit advisors may consolidate the consumer's bills into one monthly payment, they don't give loans—as debt consolidators do—or guarantee to wipe out or settle debts for not exactly the chief amount you owe.

However, the fact that credit guiding itself won't affect your score doesn't mean that enrolling in a credit advisor's debt management plan will leave your credit sound. A few lenders will report you as late only for enrolling in a debt management plan. Their thinking is that you're not paying them what you initially owed, so you ought to need to endure some agony. That is not, by any means, the only way you could be reported late.

Not all credit instructors are made equivalent, and some have been blamed for retaining consumer payments that were proposed for creditors.

I promise you: as soon as you start taking care of your money, it will pay you back.

So pay yourself first: Save and then we'll take care of the rest!

Chapter 11.

Credit Bureau and Credit Errors

How Do Credit Bureaus Gather the Information?

1. Information Supplied by Your Creditors

Usually, without your consent, your creditors send your credit information to credit bureaus. These records are sent in a format that you don't have to know. But the essential content is the personal information with which you got the loan, the type of loan it is, the terms and conditions, and how well you have played it by the book.

Of course, it is not a dark market, so you are expected to know that they send this information to credit bureaus. It is only ironic that these same credit bureaus pay to access the information.

2. Purchased Information

By legal standards, some information isn't accessible to the public. They are considered confidential, not illegal. Due to the legitimacy of credit bureaus, they often access such information, but as you guess, they part with some dough in turn. This sort of information mostly contains public records, judgments, et cetera. You can be sure credit bureaus are not interested in your personal life, adventures, or such data that are not relevant to your credits, not even your entire finances.

3. Information from Other Credit Bureaus

Despite being competitors, credit bureaus are mandated to share information sometimes. Not all the time, since each one paid to obtain their data. But sensitive data about your credits are exchanged. For example, one updates the others the instant a fraud alert was raised, or attempts were made to hack your credit report, etc.

There it is! You now understand how consumer reporting agencies gather your data and how it is being used. The next thing we should be talking about is the errors that can be found on your credit report. But before that, you should meet three major credit bureaus.

You need to have some idea who you are getting your credit reports from. Right? Entirely logical. Let's latch onto that then.

What Are the Errors That You Should Check Out in Your Credit Report?

1. Personality Identity Information

Any slack can lead to errors. So, your full name should be spelled and arranged correctly. The same thing about your Social Security Number.

How about your address? Your date of birth too. For instance, if you have earlier raised a fraud alert, security freeze, statement of dispute, etc. Whatsoever you have raised earlier, and you find documented, be sure that is exactly what you have here.

2. Credit Account History

This is the most essential part of the whole credit report, as we have earlier disclosed. You may want to pay close attention to every detail provided here, from the reports of lenders on the transaction you have had with them, to the type of transaction stated that you have had.

You also want to check their reports on the agreed duration, the duration you paid, your credit limit, your payment pattern, history, et cetera. Data as simple as account name and number should be doubly verified.

I'll be quick to add that a leak is possible from anywhere, your credit union, credit card issuer, or your credit bureau themselves.

3. Credit Inquiries

Only creditors to whom you apply for a loan can automatically request your report. The list of the inquirers and the type of credit you're hoping to have with them are displayed here.

You want to make sure that a stranger or an unknown company hasn't woken up one day to start gathering data on your credits. The moment you find one of those, you have got something to fix on your credit.

4. Public Records

To cap this, you need to scan through your public records too. We know that bad records don't help anyone, and it can't be exciting to find strange ones in your report.

If one of your credit records is overdue for removal, there is no reason you should still have it there. For the records that are still to be reflected, you want to make sure they are not understated or exaggerated. Inconsistency and inaccuracy can give you a bad light in front of every creditor.

There we are! You have just taken a tour of the Credit Bureaus and the errors you may pick out on your credit report. With that last lesson in mind, let's see about fixing your credit reports!

How Can You Get a Free Credit Report?

If you are reading this from any other part of the world, I hate to say you'd have to consult something else. Perhaps your government service, a credit officer, or anything. But if you are wondering how to do it in the U.S., it is laid on the lines here.

You need to remember that if you are checking a similar site and not exactly this, you may be charged at some point, or worst, you might be playing into a fraudster's net.

Right after filling in the personal data, pick your preferred credit report (whether Equifax, Experian, or Trans Union). On the next display, you verify your identity by answering a few questions that are directly related to your credit history. Then, your credit report is displayed on the screen.

You can simply print or return to view. Right-on. If this is not, consider calling 1-877-322-8228 and go through a similar process over the phone. You'd have to wait for a couple of weeks or one more before receiving your credit report.

Check Out Your Credit Report

Chapter 12.

How Fast and How Many Points Will a Credit Score Improve

Realistic Time Frame for a Noticeable Improvement

As mentioned, there are many steps you can take to improve your credit score. By paying off any credit card debt, disputing any errors in the report, or by even paying off any collection accounts, you can significantly improve your credit score. You must take steps to increase the positive information, reduce the negative impact, or a combination of the two in the credit report.

By doing this, you can start seeing an improvement in your credit score within a couple of weeks. For instance, by doing something as simple as making monthly payments on time, you can improve your credit score. It would help if you did this consistently, as it isn't a one-time thing. You can see an improvement in your credit score within weeks, but for a significant change, that will take a couple of months at least. Here are three factors that define the time frame for improving your credit score:

The First Factor Is the Starting Point

It takes at least a month to develop your credit score on your own. If you are trying to repair your credit, then it will take longer. For instance, if you are eligible only for a secured credit card and have damaged credit, then it can take anywhere between 12 and 18 months to improve the credit score.

The time frame will depend on how responsibly you use the approved card. The amount of pre-existing negative and positive information in your credit report will also influence this time frame.

The Second Factor Relates to the Punctuality of Your Monthly Payments

Your credit score depends on the compilation of information in the credit report. To repair damaged credit, you must keep adding positive information to the report every month. It means that you must pay all your bills, including any credit card bills or monthly repayment of a loan on time.

If you do this consistently for a couple of months, it will improve your credit rating. Also, if you have a credit card, try not to max it and instead use it wisely. Maintaining a healthy level of utilization can add positive points to your credit score.

The Third Factor Is to Define What Improvement Means to You

You will start to see your credit rate improving by a few points in a couple of weeks while it takes a couple of months to see your score change from bad to good. So, your perception of what improvement means matters while repairing your damaged credit.

At times, a minor mistake like maxing out the credit card limit or missing a payment can damage your credit. Some might be trying to recover from things they didn't realize could harm their credit like applying for a new credit card or closing an account.

Others might be dealing with more significant issues like bankruptcy. Depending on the reason that led to the depreciation of their credit rating, the time taken to get back on track will vary.

You might not have realized it, but whenever you apply for a new line of credit or close an existing account, it reduces your credit rating. The damage in such instances is minor, and the recovery time is around three months. Some major issues severely damage your credit ratings like defaulting on payments and bankruptcy.

The average recovery time for bankruptcy is over six years. You can fix the damage from defaulting on payment within two years. Then there are moderate issues like maxing out the credit card and the recovery time for these issues is three months or more.

These are just examples of how long it can take and isn't a precise estimate. The period of recovery also depends on the other information present on the credit report. Apart from this, the amount of positive and negative information on the credit report influences the recovery time. If you have a solid credit history, then it is easier to fix a misstep.

However, if your credit report is riddled with mistakes, it will become quite challenging to repair. The lower your credit score, the lesser ground you have to cover, and the easier it is to improve the score.

For instance, A and B have both defaulted on their mortgage payments. A has a credit score of 780, while B's credit score is only 680. A will take anywhere between 3 and 7 years to repair the score while B can repair it within ten months. Improving your credit score isn't a one-time thing, it is a continuous process.

The addition of information to the credit report will keep altering the credit score. Your financial goals, along with your existing financial position, are two factors that influence your need to improve the credit score.

What Impacts a Credit Report?

From a lender's perspective, the following points are positive items on a credit report:

- If you pay your bills on time and do so consistently.

- Have been and still can maintain a reasonable balance of unused credit.

- Apply for credit only when the need arises. When you do this, the number of inquiries against you is to a bare minimum.

- Consistently check your annual credit reports and correct any mistakes in them.

- Certain red flags that a potential lender looks for in a borrower's credit report include the following.

As you can see, different factors influence your credit score. Every financial transaction that you make impacts your annual credit report. Paying your monthly cable bill might be a small transaction, but it does affect your credit report.

If you consistently pay your monthly utility bills, it will help improve your credit score. However, if you get behind on payments or miss due dates on monthly utility bills, then it will significantly decrease your credit score. If your credit score is less than 579, then you will be viewed as a risky borrower by the lenders. A score of 582 to 669 might qualify you for approval of loans from some vendors.

A good credit score is between 670 and 739. You are a dependable borrower if your score is higher than 740. You qualify as an exceptional borrower if your credit score is more than 800.

Why No One Can Guarantee an Increase in Points

As mentioned earlier, your credit score is a three-digit number. Not just banks and lenders, but several other companies have also started using credit score as a measure of your ability to repay a debt. Equifax, Trans Union, and Experian are the three main credit bureaus that create all the credit reports. Vantage Score and The Fair Isaac Co-operation (FICO) are credit scoring models that then use the information given in the credit reports for coming up with an individual's credit score. The credit score is usually in the range of 300 to 850.

The credit bureaus might also, at times, generate credit scores based on some other proprietary model. The credit score is calculated based on different things like the frequency of payments, duration of the accounts, or the expenditure you incur, and so on. Credit scores aren't influenced by personal demographics like sex, age, religion, nationality, or marital status.

There are different ways in which credit scores are calculated, and therefore, it is not unusual to have multiple scores simultaneously. Your credit scores depend on the bureau or the agencies that the specific lender reports. For instance, a lender might report to two agencies.

You can have multiple credit scores if a lender doesn't report to all three agencies at the same time. Apart from this, the lending situation can also mean that you have different scores. For instance, the credit model used by a mortgage lender will be different from that used by other lenders.

Regardless of the model used, these scores are based on all the information present in the credit report.

However, the formula that is used for obtaining these credit scores is closely guarded much like the fried chicken recipe at KFC or the formula used in Coca-Cola. Certain factors have a positive or negative influence on your credit rating. If you look at all the information that is available online, you will notice that you can certainly improve your credit rating by following specific steps. The one thing that no one guarantees is the number of points that are associated with each factor that influences the credit score.

It is safe to assume that not paying your cable bill for six months will hurt your credit score. However, it isn't possible to estimate the number of points you will lose when you get behind on your payments.

This estimation isn't possible because the formula used for calculating the score is safely guarded. Apart from this, the effect that a specific factor has on one's credit score also depends on their existing credit score.

◆ ◆ ◆

Make Sure You Can Limit as Much as Possible
the Hard Inquiries to Get the Best Results with This

Chapter 13. Techniques to Rebuild your Credit

Pay Off What You Owe

While this is going to be easier said than done in most situations, according to Experian, the ideal amount of credit utilization that you want is 30% or less. While there are other ways to increase your credit utilization rating, paying off what you owe on time each month will also go towards showing you can pay your bills on time, essentially pulling double duty when it comes to improving your credit score. It will also make it easier to follow through on the following tips.

Pay Your Credit Card Bills Twice a Month

If you have a credit card that you use regularly, say, for example, because it offers you reward points, so much so that you max it out each month, it may actually be hurting your credit even though you pay it off in full at the end of each month. This may be the case due to the way the credit card company reports to the credit bureau; depending on when they report each month it could show that your credit utilization rate is close to 100% depending on what your credit line currently is, thus hurting your credit score. As such, paying off your credit card in two smaller chunks throughout the month can actually help boost your credit without costing you anything extra overall.

Increase Your Credit Limit

If you aren't currently able to pay down your credit card balance, you can still improve your credit utilization rate by increasing your current credit limit. This is an easy way to improve your credit utilization rate without putting any more money out upfront. If you do this, however, you mustn't take advantage of the increased credit line as if you find yourself up against the limit again you will be worse off than when you started. Only pursue this option if you have the willpower to avoid racking up extra charges, especially if you are already strapped when it comes to the payments you need to make each month; decreasing your credit utilization limit while also making more late payments is a lateral move at best.

Open a New Account

Improving your credit utilization rate is one of the best ways to start rebuilding your credit. If your current credit card company won't increase your credit limit, you may try applying for another credit card instead. If your credit is not so hot, then your rates are going to be higher, but this won't matter as long as you don't plan on using the card in the first place. Remember, the credit utilization rate is a combination of your total available lines of credit so this can be a good way to drop your current utilization rate substantially, especially if you won't be able to pay off what you currently owe for a significant time.

However, keep in mind that if you choose this route, then you are only going to apply for one new card every couple of months, especially if you aren't sure if you are going to be approved, as too many hard credit inquiries will only cause your credit score to drop, even if you do end up with a better credit utilization rate as a result. Spreading out these requests will give the inquiries time to drop off naturally and will prevent you from looking desperate to potential lenders, which can also make it more difficult to get a new card.

Authorized Users

If you don't have the credit to get a new credit card, or even to extend your current credit line, then your best choice may be to find someone you trust and ask them to become an authorized user on their card. While most people will likely balk at the idea, you may be able to pacify them by explaining that you don't need a copy of their card or have any intent on using it, simply being listed on the card is enough to improve your credit utilization rating. Not only that, but you will also get credit for the on-time payments that this other person makes.

Chapter 14..

Resolving Bad Credit Situation

Most people who are regarded as a bad credit risk are likely to be shut out by the same society, which flourishes on credit. You may find this such a huge contradiction. Being marked as having bad credit may result in having deep internal wounds. This is because, naturally, you would not want your neighbors to find out about your bad credit. Worse, it would be a dishonor on your part if your entire community would find out and be the topic of their gossips.

In reality, you do not have to deal with this type of mentality even if you have a bad credit situation. This issue is only a result of exaggeration from federal authorities and financial institutions that almost 40% to 45% of the people are in a bad credit situation. On the other hand, you need to understand that having bad credit is not the end of the world. Bad credit only implies that future financial institutions will be careful when carrying out transactions with you. For instance, you may be obliged to pay earlier than you used to, which is to be expected. Besides, if you were in the shoes of these financial institutions, you would also do the same.

Fortunately, there are several enterprises and people who are adept at repairing a bad credit situation. Furthermore, there are books, e-books, videos, DVDs, and CDs that can educate you about various credit situations.

If you are already in a situation of bad credit, it is best to use real money when purchasing instead of plastic, such as credit cards. This can help you spend less, and you will be inclined to avoid even the most effective marketing strategies of companies. You need to get a hold of yourself by learning the techniques and tools on how you can cope with your bad credit situation. The key is to fight the situation to restore your good financial state as well as your dignity.

Some Simple Tips on Resolving a Bad Credit Situation

Probably the worst situation that a credit card holder would be in is a bad credit situation. Apart from hindering one's current life, it can also affect the potential of applying for or securing a loan.

Several factors may lead to a bad credit situation. The most common of which is overspending. This is considered as the most considerable factor that results in a bad credit situation.

Another factor is the non-payment on time. Often, people, especially credit card holders, neglect paying on time for their different purchases, which later affect their credit history.

Inevitable conditions such as unemployment, health problems, and financial setbacks also lead to having a bad credit situation. These are conditions wherein people are left with no choice but to spend without considering their credit scores.

Fortunately, there are various ways to improve your credit score through proper rules, which can help you resolve your situation on time. First, you can check for the consistency of your credit report. This will ensure that no wrong information and mistakes are included in your report. Should there be any inaccuracy, make sure to report it at once to the concerned credit bureau or creditor to carry out the necessary correction.

Second, it is best to keep a budget for your expenses. This involves discerning the items that contributed considerably to your bad credit rating. It also involves saving money to repay debts and controlling yourself on overspending.

Third, set an appointment with your creditors and request a plan through which you can pay your debt appropriately. It is best to consult them in establishing the plan so that you can effectively pay your debt.

Fourth, you can ask for counseling from various organizations to improve your bad credit rating. These organizations can carry out negotiations with your creditors by convincing the latter to lower the interest rate and create a repayment plan for you.

Fifth, make sure to inform your creditors in advance if you are going to skip a repayment. However, it is best to avoid skipping payments, since it would not always be in your favor.

Finally, make sure you are determined to follow the repayment plan that your creditor has provided for you. It is best not to play around with your creditors, especially when they have given you the chance to repay your debt in the most convenient way.

Important Steps to Take Towards Credit Repair

By now, you should already know how credit serves as an important tool in your life. For one, many things having a good credit rating allows you to have. These include being able to rent a house or property, having a credit card, and qualifying for in-store financing, among others. When you have a poor credit rating, it is advisable to take the necessary steps to repair it. However, the process of repairing credit is usually slow and necessary for rebuilding your credit rating over time. Fortunately, there are some tips that you can follow to start the credit repair process as soon as possible.

First, you can add accounts to your credit report. Then, check for errors or discrepancies. If there are none, this means your credit rating is "poor" because your credit history is insufficient to reflect a good rating and not due to outstanding debts.

There are types of credit that credit bureaus do not track. These credit types usually come from small organizations. For instance, department store cards or gas cards are not included in your credit report. If you add these accounts to your credit report, you can rebuild a good credit rating. Thus, you should ask the concerned credit bureau to track these accounts. However, most credit bureaus ask for an additional service fee when adding types of credit from small organizations. Only verifiable accounts are usually tracked by credit bureaus and added to your file free of charge.

Second, you can seek the help of a credit counselor. When you become entangled in debt, it can be difficult to come out of it, especially if it has already fed on itself. This means that your original debt amount has gone higher due to its interest. Furthermore, if you find it taxing to carry out a credit repair on your own or continually encounter problems during the process of credit repair, you should consult a credit counseling agency.

There is a huge difference between a credit counseling company and a credit repair company. Credit counseling companies are non-profit services that offer guidance and advice on how to do a credit repair, while credit repair companies are for-profit organizations that charge fees for taking steps for repairing your credit; however, these steps are not necessarily legal or particularly conscious about ethics.

You can tell if you have found a good credit counselor when he/she can make a realistic budget to which you can stick to as well as help in making practical decisions about your debts.

By adding accounts to your credit report and consulting a credit counselor as necessary, you can make the process of credit repair easy. Make sure that the account that you will add to your credit report is in good standing.

Keep in mind that it can take a long time to obtain a good credit rating and an extremely short period to destroy it. Once your credit rating is damaged, you need to accept that there is no quick way to repair it. You will be obliged to rebuild your good credit standing from scratch. As such, you need to avoid the promises of credit repair companies that they have quick and easy solutions for a fee. An intelligent and practical way of repairing your credit is to improve your budgeting as well as spending habits.

Conclusion

The fact that you made it here goes a long way to show how serious you are about getting the credit score you desire. However, remember that it is not possible to enhance your credit score overnight. But by following the information in this book and implementing it the right way, you will start to see your credit rating go up.

No one who is starting out in life expects to find themselves in financial turmoil. However, for most people, it will happen at some point during our adult lives.

The three-digit FICO score can have a stronger impact on our future than any other grade we get in our lives. Yet, no matter how bad it seems, there is no point where it can't be turned around and improved.

The reality is that we live in a society that almost demands that we have some form of credit, not to get ahead, but simply to survive. When we are without it, we suffer in more ways than one.

What better reason is there to start mending our financial health than this? Yes, it can be scary, unpredictable, and stressful, but by applying the strategies outlined in this book, you can find your way to a successful credit repair without the additional expense of hiring services to do it for you.

There is an excellent benefit to fixing your credit yourself. Not only do you save yourself from an additional expense when you are already financially strapped, but you become an expert and play a major starring role in your own life.

As you can see, your credit score has a lot more to it than you think. It is one of the most important things to have control of to live a better life. Not only will great credit provide you with a sense of pride, but it will also allow you to do the things and buy the things that you want. We all dream of a certain home or car. Make that dream a reality with good responsible habits.

One of those habits is working on your credit. Now, many things go along with credit when it comes to being successful. Having an excellent credit score will save you a lot of pain and emotional stress. Great credit will get you one step closer to living the life you want to live—a life of financial stability and happiness.

Maybe you are seeking to rebuild your credit score, I have given out some tips needed on how to improve your credit scores, basics of credit repair, how you could repair your credit, the FICO score, and how credit cards could affect your scores. However, you need to take action to get the desired results.

If you are in debt or you are struggling with bad credit, this book opens you to ten steps that could be taken as a road towards getting 100 points in

30 days. Pleasure is far from the reason for writing this book. But the book was written to guide, direct, and inspire you in taking the needed actions to improve yourself as an individual. Your success is thus dependent on the practical actions you employ to improve yourself.

I hope this book helps you on your journey to better credit. But my main hope is to help anyone out there who is struggling to achieve greatness. With the power of the mind, anything is possible. Now get out there and increase your credit.

Dave R. W. Graham

Author's Note

Thanks for reading my book. If you want to learn more about personal finance, investments, trading, and business, I suggest you follow my author page on Amazon. Through my books, I have decided to share with you the know-how that has allowed me to achieve my financial freedom, accumulate wealth, and live the life I want with my family.

My goal is to show you the path for reaching your targets, with useful and applicable information. Only you will be able to tread that path as I did… and now, I'm sharing what I know.

Thank you for your time, and **if you enjoyed this book I will appreciate one honest review of yours.** *This will help me to improve my upcoming work on these topics, so I can more effectively share my knowledge and my story with other readers.*

To your wealth!

Dave R. W. Graham